ISBN: 978-1-716-39434-8

Cover Illustration: inside a hard drive

Release date: June 16, 2017

Language: English, translated from French by DeepL

Backup your files

Lionel Bolnet

Author and self-publisher:

Lionel Bolnet

Distributor:

www.lulu.com

The science of "Backupology"

"Still not well known by the general public, computer backup is a rapidly growing field that echoes the increase in data loss by companies and individuals. For companies, the issue is commercial, while for individuals it is a sentimental one."

Lionel Bolnet

Table of contents

Introduction

Files are everywhere. Still non-existent in your life, in the 90s, files have become ubiquitous: located in your cell phone, on your desktop computer, on your tablet, in your game consoles, in your televisions, in the Internet service provider's box, in your camera, in your camcorder and even in your car.

All these files contain intimate, artistic, confidential, professional, administrative elements... They are virtual and their existence depends only on the material support on which they are recorded. Thus, the threats of the physical world hover over the files of the virtual world. The threats are the risks incurred by these physical supports. They are innumerable, but they include: theft, breakage, wear and tear, fire, loss.

Nowadays, in the event of a hardware disaster of a computer equipment, merchants are happy to help you re-equip by selling you a new device. But no one seems to care about the files that were on it. It's up to you, the user, to worry about this loss. But often the damage is done: a lost file is often lost forever. Depending on the cause of the loss, you may turn to data recovery companies, but the result is not guaranteed and, of course, impossible in case of loss or theft of the device. Recovery is a technique that involves trying to recover deleted data from a healthy or damaged storage medium.

Backup is a **preventive procedure that** aims to anticipate the recovery work the day a data loss problem occurs.

As long as no problems occur, it falsely gives the impression of being useless...

Why do we need to back up?

A survey by data protection specialist Acronis showed in 2015 that less than half of computer users back up their duplicate files.

This means that one out of every two people is not afraid of losing their files, or thinks it will never happen. This is the application of the adage "it only happens to others".

In fact, you MUST back up your data for several reasons. First of all, there is currently no computer support that guarantees 100% data retention reliability. That is to say that no device on the market is capable of ensuring that nothing will erase your data. For example, hard disks, which represent the cornerstone of file storage in the world (in 2017), are robust yet breakable devices: they are metal cases containing disks surmounted by electromechanical arms. By dropping them more than two meters high, they are certain to break, losing their data.

Figure 1 : A hard-disk drive is a device made of rigid aluminum, ceramic or glass platters. Therefore, they can break.

Dropping on the floor is not the only danger to a hard drive: hard drives can also be destroyed by excessive heat or humidity. Indeed, a hard drive immersed in water will have very little chance of re-functioning. Following these three types of disasters, you can take the defective hard drive to a data recovery lab: these companies make every effort to unscrew the hard drives in order to restore as much data as possible. Of course, sometimes nothing can be recovered.

Let's take the example of another medium: SD cards found in cameras are so fragile that if you break them by bending them in half with your teeth, their contents will be completely erased.

Figure 2 : Just like hard drives, SD cards are not immortal. They can be broken, burned. On the other hand, they are highly resistant to moisture and frost.

In addition to these causes of hardware destruction, there are also causes of software destruction. Even if a storage medium is in good shape, the files it contains can be victim of voluntary or involuntary loss or deletion.

Figure 3 : Illustration of "computer rage", a tantrum caused by computers.

You've probably already pulled your hair out by repeating "oh no, oh no, oh no no no no" when you find that you've inadvertently deleted or modified a file. If, moreover, this file is a 145-page document that you have just written and that nobody in the world has a copy of it, the disaster is total. There is a multitude of risks of involuntary deletion or modification:

- A child playing on an adult's computer,
- A file that you delete without asking your spouse's permission,
- A virus that encrypts all your files.

Viruses that encrypt all files are becoming more and more common. The year 2017 saw the spread of this type of virus, which is called "ransomware". The principle is Machiavellian: when your computer is infected by ransomware, it starts to encrypt all your files with a password that you will be unable to guess. Everything is encrypted: MP3s, photos, videos of the kids at Disneyland, scanned pay slips, PDFs, Excel documents to send to your boss the next day first thing in the morning?

The pirates used a loophole discovered by the American intelligence services. 150 countries were affected. In France, where Renault was forced to stop production at certain sites, the public prosecutor's office opened an investigation.

Hackers have apparently exploited a loophole in Windows systems, disclosed in hacked documents from the U.S. security agency NSA. This gave Edward Snowden the opportunity to further castigate his former employer. [...] Shortly after this loophole was made public, Microsoft released a fix to prevent attacks, but many systems were clearly not updated by their users, which was used by hackers who saw big and wrote their ransom demand (the one that appears on the victims' screen and blocks it) in 17 languages. [...] The software used by hackers locks users' files and forces them to pay a sum of money in the form of bitcoins to recover their use. This practice is called "ransomware" and is becoming more and more common. "200,000 victims in at least 150 countries" (Director Europol): this is the latest assessment, Sunday at midday. [...]

Figure 4 : Excerpt from an article published on 13/05/2017 (on https://www.lesechos.fr)

The ransomware will then give you about 48 hours to direct you to a ransom payment website. You will then have to unlock the password that will unlock your documents. Of course, sometimes, even after the ransom has been paid, your files remain locked. It would be too easy otherwise.

Security experts are adamant: in case of a ransomware attack, you don't have to pay the ransom! On the one hand, because you wouldn't be sure to get the decryption password, and on the other hand because it will encourage other criminals to enter this niche. You need to format the infected computer, reinstall the operating system and deliver your files from their most recent uninfected backup. This is the typical "reinstall from scratch" procedure.

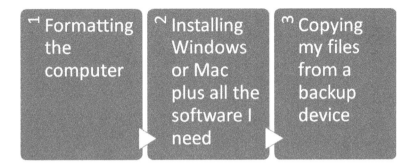

Figure 5 : To follow steps 1 and 2 of the recovery process, you may need the assistance of a computer-savvy friend or a repairman. But step 3 can only be done by you, provided, of course, that you have a backup.

What should be backed up?

Once you are convinced that you need to back up your files, the next question is what perimeter to protect. Back up with care: not too much, not too little.

In a computer, there are two types of:

- "System" files.
- "User" files.

System Backup

System files are those that allow the operating system (Windows, MacOS, etc...) to work. They are important, but backing them up means knowing how to restore them in case of a disaster. You recognize system files by their little-known extensions such as ".ini", ".exe", ".dll", ".inf".

But you can also find them in the Windows directories where you never browse:

- C:\Program Files
- C:\Program Files (x86)
- C:\Windows

Should they be backed up? Yes. You can save them but be careful: it is generally advisable not to touch these files. It's better not to read or modify them.

Moreover, if you save them by simple copy and paste, it does not mean at all that you will be able to reinstall Windows or a program from their backup. System files are more complicated than that.

Backing up your system means creating an accurate image of the computer you are using so that you can get it back on its feet if one day it becomes infested with viruses or is completely emptied of its contents for any reason. Backing up your system includes both system files and user files.

The following tutorial only concerns computers running Windows 7, 8 or 10.

First of all, what will the "system image" be used for? Maybe it will never be used or maybe it will save you a lot of hassle. In fact, the system image is a backup of your entire computer from A to Z.

If you are reading this paragraph, I advise you to schedule a backup session of your system image in the next few days.

Step 1: Free up disk space by deleting what is unnecessary in your computer. For example, empty the recycle bin, uninstall programs that are useless. All this is to reduce the future size of the system image that you plan to build.

Second step: it is advisable to run a complete scan of your system with an antivirus. It would be a shame to create a system image with a virus inside. Otherwise the wolf would be in the sheepfold on the day your computer is restored.

Step 3: Take an external storage medium such as an external hard drive, a large USB stick or blank DVDs and insert it into the computer to be backed up. Buy another one if its capacity is too small.

Let's now move on to the creation of the system image.

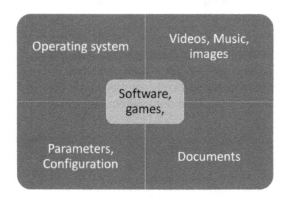

Figure 6 : The system image will probably weigh a lot! It will contain absolutely the whole of your computer in a usable format in case of restoration.

Go to the tool proposed by Windows with these steps: Control Panel > System and Security > Backup and Restore (Windows 7).

Figure 7 : Control Panel view

Then click on "Create a system image".

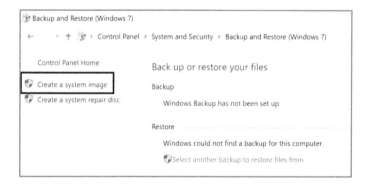

Figure 8 : The Backup and Restore tool. It is also named "Windows 7" which is pretty confusing considering this capture has been done on Windows 10.

It is time for you to plug in any USB device you want to use for this backup: USB flash drive, external SSD, external hard-disk drive.

Windows will now automatically search for external devices i.e. any storage media that is not the current partition of your Windows system (i.e. everything except the C:/ partition). Among the propositions, choose well the storage medium you want. Make sure it has enough capacity, i.e. a capacity close to what your C: partition occupies.

Figure 9 : Selection of the device to store the backup

It is not recommended to save your system image to another partition of the same internal disk. Indeed, how could this disk help you if the whole computer is flooded with viruses or if it perishes in some accident? Be wise: choose an **external** device.

Then Windows will ask you which partitions you want to save. One or more of them will already be checked and impossible to uncheck. It is advisable to check the others as well.

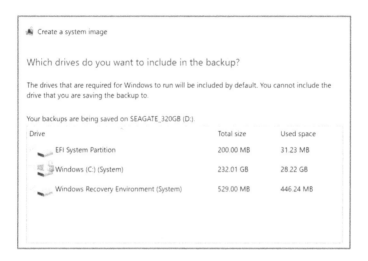

Figure 10 : Selection of drives to backup

At this point Windows calculates for you the space required and the space available to perform the operation. This is indicated at the bottom of the frame. If the required space is less than the available space, the operation is feasible.

Click Next to see the confirmation window:

Figure 11 : Confirmation

Now, think carefully about what you are doing because the operation will take a long time, so if it's not the right time, postpone it to another time.

Then, when you are ready, click "Start Backup". Now be patient.

Figure 12 : Wait for the end of the backup. It can last several minutes, or even hours.

Once the system image is created, you will see this:

Figure 13 : The end

Windows asks you a tricky question. They ask whether you want to create a boot disc. In my opinion, this question is particularly stupid. Firstly, system repair disc can be done at any other moment. Secondly, many computers do not own a CD burner. So, it might end like this:

Create a system repair disc

The system repair disc could not be
created

Windows did not find a CD/DVD burner. If you do
have a CD/DVD burner, make sure it is connected to
the computer and try again.

OK

Figure 14 : This message is not important at all. It just means that you don't have a CD burner. Remember that this tool developed at a time where CDs were common.

On your selected media, you will be able to see the existence of a new folder named WindowsImageBackup. If you enter it, you won't see anything usual as files. Those files are the image of your system. You cannot open them.

Name	Date	Type	Size
4bb23229-a07b-4147-99ee-e838463cb8a9.v...	24/11/2020 18:57	Archivo de imagen	485.376 KB
a1b33ae0-41c3-4246-bb25-446904b77508.v...	24/11/2020 18:57	Archivo de imagen...	25.315.328 KB
BackupSpecs.xml	24/11/2020 18:57	Documento XML	2 KB
ceb87ddf-0a5c-4add-bb13-187456e01cc0_...	24/11/2020 18:57	Documento XML	1 KB
ceb87ddf-0a5c-4add-bb13-187456e01cc0_...	24/11/2020 18:57	Documento XML	17 KB
ceb87ddf-0a5c-4add-bb13-187456e01cc0_...	24/11/2020 18:57	Documento XML	7 KB
ceb87ddf-0a5c-4add-bb13-187456e01cc0_...	24/11/2020 18:57	Documento XML	9 KB
ceb87ddf-0a5c-4add-bb13-187456e01cc0_...	24/11/2020 18:57	Documento XML	2 KB
ceb87ddf-0a5c-4add-bb13-187456e01cc0_...	24/11/2020 18:57	Documento XML	2 KB
ceb87ddf-0a5c-4add-bb13-187456e01cc0_...	24/11/2020 18:57	Documento XML	3 KB
ceb87ddf-0a5c-4add-bb13-187456e01cc0_...	24/11/2020 18:57	Documento XML	9 KB
ceb87ddf-0a5c-4add-bb13-187456e01cc0_...	24/11/2020 18:57	Documento XML	6 KB
ceb87ddf-0a5c-4add-bb13-187456e01cc0_...	24/11/2020 18:57	Documento XML	8.138 KB
Esp.vhdx	24/11/2020 18:57	Archivo de imagen...	57.344 KB

Figure 15 : Files contained in WindowsImageBackup

This operation of system image creation must be performed regularly because, from month to month, from year to year, the system image will perish, i.e. its content will be further and further away from the real content of your computer. So, try to schedule this kind of operation from time to time.

Backup of user files

Unlike system files, user files are the ones you view and modify on a daily basis. They can be classified in 4 sub-categories:

- The videos
- The music,
- The pictures,
- The documents.

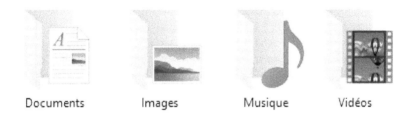

Documents   Images   Musique   Vidéos

Figure 16 : You can broadly classify your files into four sub-categories. If your files are not well arranged in these 4 folders, it is advisable to clean up a bit before thinking about backing up.

Let's now focus on the backup of user files. These are files that are important and valuable to you for a variety of reasons:

Photos are generally irreplaceable. Nowadays, few people keep all their photos in paper and cardboard photo albums as they did in the past. Since the advent of digital cameras, overwhelmed by the vast number of digital photographs, most people keep their photos only in electronic format. These photos can have a very strong emotional and sentimental importance. This is why saving photographs is a major issue.

Someone steals her computer with photos of her dead husband: her family makes a call on Facebook.

The family of a nurse hopes to recover a stolen computer in Roubaix. It contains precious photos: those of her recently deceased husband. On Sunday, the niece of the victim of the theft launched this call on Facebook (it was relayed by La Voix du Nord). Objective: to find the computer stolen Sunday evening in her car that was parked on Rue de l'Espérance, near the La Piscine museum in Roubaix. The nurse made the mistake of leaving her computer in the car. "The windows are tinted," she explained to the journalist. In the stolen Macbook, there are photos of her husband, who died three months ago. Precious memories that she would like to be able to keep. It also contains courses to review for upcoming exams. "It's my whole life," the victim says in the regional daily newspaper. [...]

Figure 17 : Excerpt from an article published on 04/04/2017 (on http://france3-regions.francetvinfo.fr/)

For videos and music, however, the case is different. Rare are the videos or pieces of music that have sentimental value. In fact, with the decline of the camcorder, the tendency to store family videos has greatly diminished. But it doesn't matter how many of them there are: they should also be backed up. On the other hand, it is still possible to have a nice MP3 or DIVX media library. Losing these files would be like losing a CD or DVD collection. Since the democratization of VOD, legal streaming, Spotify, YouTube, etc., the current era is not very conducive to the storage of music and video files. But if you have them, maybe you want to keep them in a safe place.

Documents in the broadest sense are all text file formats such as Word, Excel, Powerpoint, HTML or PDF. They are usually typed on the keyboard. Their importance varies from one file to another. These files may well have sentimental value (such as a scanned letter or a self-composed poem). And they can also be important for an administrative (pay slip, tax notice, proof of address, invoices) or professional (report, technical file, etc...) reason.

Finally, even though this technology is of little interest to many users, BitCoin is a monetary currency that has only a digital existence. This currency is stored inside an electronic wallet saved in a file with the extension ".dat". These files then have a real monetary value.

By throwing away his old computer, he loses more than 7 million dollars in Bitcoin.

When he threw his hard drive in the trash, James Howells didn't imagine that one day it would be worth millions... For the man, who works in high-tech, it was just an old piece of a computer on which he had spilled a drink. The hard drive had been sitting in a drawer in his desk for three years, while the other parts of the machine that could have any value had been resold. James Howells had ended up forgetting even its contents, "distracted by family life and a move," he told the BBC. In 2013, sorting through all his old technology, he threw it away without a second thought, thinking he had already saved the essential data. [...]

Figure 18 : Excerpt from an article published on 29/11/2013 (on http://www.latribune.fr)

Beyond music, videos, photos and office documents, only the user of a computer can know what is valuable to them and therefore needs to be backed up. For example:

- Contact directory cards,

- E-mails,
- Favourite URLs,
- BitCoin,
- 3D objects,
- Video game games.

If you are using a computer running Windows 10, you can see the file categories predefined by Microsoft in the directory with your username:

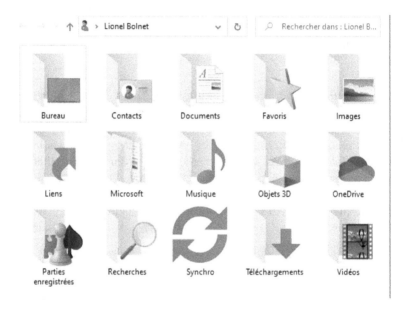

Figure 19 : Windows suggests the tree structure you may use

When should I back up?

A backup is a photograph of your files at a given moment. Your files live on your computer. Every day, you create them, you modify them, you delete them, you move them, you rename them. The more time elapses between the last backup and the present, the more the backup will be considered obsolete.

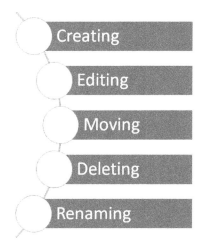

Figure 20 : The five actions that make your files "alive"

The regularity with which you back up your files is called the backup frequency. It is up to you to choose it keeping in mind these two principles:

- **A too high** backup frequency consumes a lot of IT resources, i.e. disk space, network bandwidth, RAM, and hard disk speed. In simple terms, we can say that with each backup, you will probably slow down your entire computer and network connection.

- **A too low** backup frequency, on the other hand, will not protect you sufficiently in case of data recovery. For example, if you back up your files every 2nd of the month and your computer crashes on the 22nd, your backup won't contain what you've been doing for 20 days!

It is therefore a trade-off between resources and the need to be up to date that everyone must reflect on.

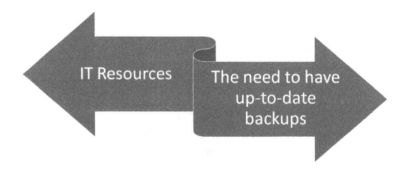

Figure 21 : Choose wisely your backup frequency

Note that high frequency is desirable but difficult to achieve in some cases. For example, in the case of backup to an external hard disk connected to USB, backup can be performed only every time the user plugs in the external hard disk. Under these very "manual" conditions, it is hard to imagine a backup frequency greater than once a day.

With some technologies, for example the cloud, it is possible to obtain a permanent backup frequency, i.e. files are always backed up immediately after they are created or modified, in real time.

Hot, Warm and Cold

The files that you view and edit year-round are stored primarily on your computer: they are the originals of your digital heritage. They live, they are edited, deleted and added constantly. They can therefore be considered as "**hot**" files.

If you use an online backup solution, i.e. available at any time, via the computer network to which your computer is connected, you can set up a fairly high backup update frequency (once a day, once an hour or even in real-time). This backup, which closely follows variations of the original files, can be described as "**warm**" files. Those files are, within a few minutes or hours, identical replicas of the "hot" files.

Finally, if you save to an offline backup solution, i.e. one that is not connected to your computer network, this backup can be described as "**cold**" files or "archive". Note that the advantage of cold backup is that it cannot be infected by a virus since it is not connected to the network. It is aptly named cold: the media is not electrically connected except at the time of backups.

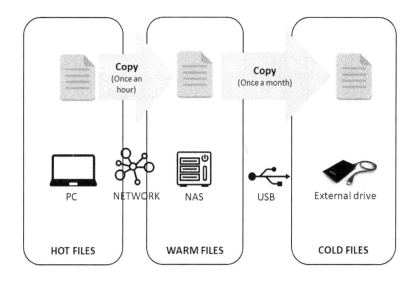

Figure 22 : Example of an installation with two backup systems only for user files. The one on the right is cold, or "an archive".

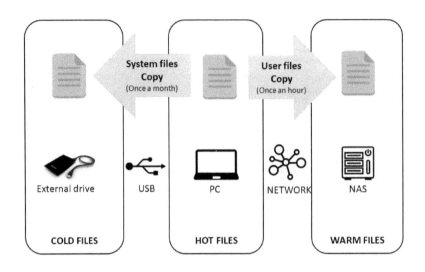

Figure 23 : Example of user and system backups

You can decide your own backup frequencies depending on your needs and your hardware. Those are examples:

NAME	SCOPE	FREQUENCY	SUPPORT
WARM BACKUP	User files only	Every hour	NAS or Cloud
COLD BCKUP	Whole system	Every month	External hard disk

Or, to be even more careful:

NAME	SCOPE	FREQUENCY	SUPPORT

WARM BACKUP	User files only	Every 15 minutes	NAS or Cloud
COLD BACKUP	Whole system	Every 10 days	External hard disk

In the case of a system backup, it is important to know that, generally those kinds of backup tend to last very long time, so almost impossible to perform multiple times per day.

The versioning

Version management is part of the art of backup. There are, in fact, two ways of backing up a file: the first consists in regularly backing up a file by deleting the previous version of this file each time. The second, more useful method consists in keeping each new version of a file, in fact, allowing the user to go back in time if he/she wishes to find what he/she is looking for in the past history of the file.

Nom	Modifié le	Type	Taille
Sauvegarder ses fichiers EN-US.docx 2020-11-21 034501.docx	20/11/2020 20:34	Document Micros...	6 383 Ko
Sauvegarder ses fichiers EN-US.docx 2020-11-21 113501.docx	21/11/2020 03:44	Document Micros...	13 184 Ko
Sauvegarder ses fichiers EN-US.docx 2020-11-21 125501.docx	21/11/2020 03:45	Document Micros...	13 184 Ko
Sauvegarder ses fichiers EN-US.docx 2020-11-23 015501.docx	21/11/2020 12:50	Document Micros...	6 591 Ko
Sauvegarder ses fichiers EN-US.docx 2020-11-23 021501.docx	23/11/2020 01:51	Document Micros...	6 591 Ko
Sauvegarder ses fichiers EN-US.docx 2020-11-23 140501.docx	23/11/2020 02:08	Document Micros...	6 591 Ko
Sauvegarder ses fichiers EN-US.docx 2020-11-23 141501.docx	23/11/2020 13:57	Document Micros...	6 592 Ko
Sauvegarder ses fichiers EN-US.docx 2020-11-23 143501.docx	23/11/2020 14:05	Document Micros...	6 592 Ko
Sauvegarder ses fichiers EN-US.docx 2020-11-23 144501.docx	23/11/2020 14:30	Document Micros...	6 591 Ko
Sauvegarder ses fichiers EN-US.docx 2020-11-23 145501.docx	23/11/2020 14:44	Document Micros...	6 461 Ko
Sauvegarder ses fichiers EN-US.docx 2020-11-23 150501.docx	23/11/2020 14:51	Document Micros...	6 460 Ko
Sauvegarder ses fichiers EN-US.docx 2020-11-23 152501.docx	23/11/2020 14:58	Document Micros...	6 460 Ko
Sauvegarder ses fichiers EN-US.docx 2020-11-23 153501.docx	23/11/2020 15:18	Document Micros...	6 278 Ko
Sauvegarder ses fichiers EN-US.docx 2020-11-23 154501.docx	23/11/2020 15:28	Document Micros...	6 212 Ko
Sauvegarder ses fichiers EN-US.docx 2020-11-23 164501.docx	23/11/2020 15:43	Document Micros...	4 441 Ko
Sauvegarder ses fichiers EN-US.docx 2020-11-23 165501.docx	23/11/2020 16:05	Document Micros...	4 441 Ko
Sauvegarder ses fichiers EN-US.docx 2020-11-23 170501.docx	23/11/2020 16:52	Document Micros...	4 187 Ko
Sauvegarder ses fichiers EN-US.docx 2020-11-23 175501.docx	23/11/2020 17:04	Document Micros...	4 187 Ko
Sauvegarder ses fichiers EN-US.docx 2020-11-24 143500.docx	23/11/2020 17:09	Document Micros...	4 188 Ko
Sauvegarder ses fichiers EN-US.docx 2020-11-24 145500.docx	24/11/2020 14:33	Document Micros...	4 231 Ko
Sauvegarder ses fichiers EN-US.docx 2020-11-24 151500.docx	24/11/2020 14:52	Document Micros...	4 249 Ko

Figure 24 : This book has been regularly saved during its writing. All the versions are kept in the backup device.

Because of versioning, one should expect a storage medium that needs more capacity than the source device of the files.

What to back up on?

Dozens of file backup media exist and have existed in the past. Let's review them.

The magnetic tape

In the history of computing, the first form of data backup media was magnetic tape.

Figure 25 : Inherited from audio magnetic tapes, computer magnetic tape still exists in 2017 as a method of backing up data, especially in banks.

Inherited from audio magnetic tapes, computer magnetic tape still exists in 2017 as a method of backing up data, especially in banks.

The computer magnetic tape, which appeared in the 1950s, had two major interests:

- For equal storage, it was considerably cheaper than hard disks.
- It resists well to time.

Indeed, from the beginning of computing, in the 1950s, it was realized that hard disks were far too expensive and stored too little information to be considered as backup media.

The operation is as follows: once a day, all computer files are copied to a reel of magnetic tape and then the tape is stored in a cabinet protected against floods, fire, mold and magnetic radiation. It is therefore a "cold" backup.

Figure 26 : Data on a tape generally comes from a hard drive

But there is a big difference between hard disks and magnetic tapes. Hard disks are online storage while magnetic tapes are offline storage.

This means that a file stored on a hard disk can, in principle, be read immediately on demand. Whereas data recorded on a tape requires first a mechanical action (which can be performed either by a person or by a robot) before its content can be read. To better understand, take the analogy between a program on Netflix and a DVD. To play a movie on Netflix, you just have to click and wait two seconds, then to play a DVD you would have to get up, look for the DVD cover on a shelf, open the cover, take out the DVD, open the player door, etc...

Tapes still exist in some sectors such as banking but are unsuitable for uses that require responsiveness such as the web, online gaming, webmail, video platforms such as YouTube, etc. ...

The floppy disk

Let's continue this history of backup media with the floppy disks.

Figure 27 : 3.5-inch floppy disks. Preferred nomadic storage format between 1984 and about 2000.

The floppy disk was a storage device used for a handful of years to save files to give to someone or save them.

Nowadays, the floppy disk no longer exists on store shelves because it suffered from several disadvantages that are unacceptable today: a storage capacity limited to 1.44 megabytes (that's about the size of a single photo taken with a smartphone these days). And above all, the floppy disk was fragile and could stop working or lose its data without any explanation.

The CD-R

One of the products that has replaced the floppy disk is the CD-R/RW, which in common parlance is the blank CD.

Figure 28 : A stack of blank CDs

The blank CD has been the storage format of a whole generation. More solid than the floppy disk, faster to read, it contained much more data than its ancestor, the floppy disk. About 700 megabytes instead of 1.44 MB.

Its period of glory is between 2000 and 2010.

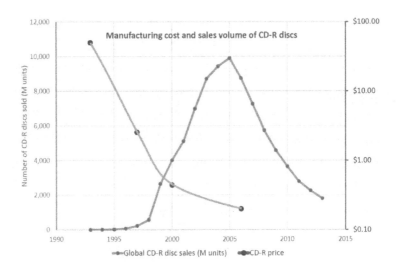

Figure 29 : The blank CD had its hour of glory in 2005: nearly 10 billion CD-Rs were burned that year.

The blank CD soon became an easy way to give a movie, a photo folder or MP3s from hand to hand. Burning a CD was a trendy gesture: teenagers were the biggest consumers. It was the transfer medium par excellence.

The CD also acted as a backup medium, because you could burn your most important files and then store the CD in a sleeve to ensure long-term preservation.

Yet scientists studying the plastic wafer were beginning to sound the alarm around the year 2000 that the physical structure of CD-R, especially entry-level CD-Rs, is not reliable enough to retain data over a long period of time.

Recordable CDs and DVDs are very bad archiving media!

We entrust them with films and photos, reports and letters, accounting and archives. Yet recordable optical discs are far from invulnerable. At the Laboratoire national de métrologie et d'essais (LNE), [...] specialists have been analyzing the wear resistance of CD-R, digital optical disks in recordable version, for several years. Presented as reliable and even strong supports, these disks, R (recordable once) or RW (rewritable at will) are indeed more resistant than the old floppy disks or magnetic tapes. These disks are ideal for monthly or yearly storage. But what about long-term archiving? How will they age? The torturers at LNE have devised all sorts of tests to simulate the outrage of years and even decades. On the menu are high, very low or highly fluctuating temperatures, extreme humidity conditions and ultraviolet floods. The results of these accelerated aging experiments were immediately rather surprising. Resistance seems to vary a lot from one brand to another but also from one model to another. High temperatures are particularly harmful, as is exposure to light. Like good wines, CD-Rs and other DVD-RWs are best stored in a cool, shady place ... LNE has also noticed that degradation is greater at the periphery of the disc (where the last recorded data is located) than near the center. In addition, the records are more damaged on the back of ink inscriptions. On the other hand, the words and drawings printed on the label can sometimes protect the data underneath... Overall, the long-term resistance appears poor. [...] The result is hardly reassuring. While audio and video CDs and DVDs keep very well, their R and RW versions would only preserve data for fifteen to twenty years for the best, the worst starting to lose it after only one year! [...]

Figure 30 : Extract from an article published on 30/04/2010 (on http://www.futura-sciences.com)

In the end, the reason for the drop in sales of CD-Rs is not linked to their supposedly bad lifespan. Simply, like the floppy disk, blank CDs have been supplanted by a subsequent invention.

The USB flash drive / USB stick

In the early 2000s, a small object gradually entered the pockets of the general public. It doesn't cost much, doesn't weigh anything, slips easily everywhere, is not fragile and is able to do what CDs can't: write, modify and delete files several times.

The very first USB flash drive came out of IBM's workshops in 2000. It could hold 8 megabytes of data, far less than a CD.

Figure 31 : Photo of the DiskOnKey, the first USB flash drive on the market.

This capacity was tiny but was simply explained: its role was not to compete with the CD but with the floppy disk. In this game, the USB flash drive was bound to win because 8 MB is more than 5 times the storage capacity of a floppy disk. The USB flash drive made it possible to record, delete, modify thousands of times without breaking down.

For the first time in the history of computing, a storage medium was neither optical nor magnetic. Indeed, the USB stick contains a memory called "flash", i.e. a memory made up of a multitude of small electronic transistors. This type of recording is particularly robust. It does not fear heat, cold, falls or magnetic radiation.

In 2017, the USB flash drive is still the object of choice for easily transporting data. Their price in 2017 is around 10€ for 16 Gigabytes of storage. The largest capacity marketed in 2017 is a 128 Gigabyte SanDisk USB flash drive at a price of only €50.

Figure 32 : SanDisk Cruzer Blade 128 GB USB 2.0 Stick

But is it an interesting backup solution?

To answer this question, we must first differentiate between the terms "backup" and "archiving". Backup is the fact of having a duplicate file (or triple, or more) in order to restore it in case of loss of the original file.

Archiving is even more delicate: it is the concept ensuring a very long conservation of a file. If you have a USB flash containing all your documents and you keep it in your bedside table, the day your computer crashes for good, you just have to take the USB flash, insert it in your new computer and that's it.

But in the long term, it is more difficult to guarantee archiving. Indeed, USB flash drives are small in size and therefore easy to lose or steal. They also have a tendency to break if they are twisted or if they are pulled out of the USB ports a bit brutally.

Figure 33 : USB flash drives can break.

Especially since manufacturers have so much wanted to lower the prices of USB sticks to democratize them, that the manufacturing materials are poorly made. Sometimes, the USB flash drive can also corrupt: it becomes unreadable without even being physically broken.

But since it is better to back up your files than to do nothing, it is a good idea to advise anyone who is afraid of one day losing their files to put them on a USB stick and keep it in a safe place.

The external hard drive

An external hard drive, as its name suggests, is a hard drive that is not inside a computer. It is usually a plastic case inside which a laptop hard drive is installed and from which comes out a cord terminated by a USB-type plug.

These devices appeared discreetly on the market when the prices of hard disks dropped and especially when the USB port became more widely available. Because without the USB port, the external hard drive could not have been invented. It was the speed of data transfer from the USB port that made the external hard drive possible.

In 2017, this kind of device will cost about 80€ for 2 terabytes (To), i.e. 2000 Gigabytes (GB).

Figure 34 : An external hard drive or SSD usually plugs into USB socket

External hard drives are actually large USB flash drives but their internal functioning is radically different: while USB flash drives contain flash memory, external hard drives contain rigid disks surmounted by mechanical arms. For this reason, they are sensitive to weather and drops. It is not advisable to drop an external hard drive on a hard surface, nor to let it stay in water or cold.

This fragility is their only big disadvantage, because for the rest, external hard drives are known to be great backup or archiving media.

Knowing that an external hard drive is guaranteed 3 years (in operation) by its manufacturer, if you use it only one hour per week to make your backups, it can theoretically live for years without causing you any problems. Provided that you do not damage it.

You must also be careful not to have it stolen. Because if you save your entire life in an external hard drive, you must make sure that no one takes your personal files. So, don't stroll an external hard drive around in the subway or leave it in plain sight on a table.

Network Attached Storage

The N.A.S. is a solution that equips more and more individuals in their homes.

A Network Attached Storage (NAS) server is a computer connected to a network whose primary function is centralized file storage.

A NAS is therefore a computer. It is not a PC (Personal Computer) because it lacks several accessories that are usually associated with a computer: it has no mouse, no keyboard, no screen, no speakers.

Figure 35 : A NAS is a computer without a screen, mouse, keyboard, and speakers.

On the other hand, a NAS does have a motherboard, a processor, RAM memory, a fan, one or more hard drives, a power supply, an Ethernet network card, and USB ports. So, a NAS is not just a device. It is a stand-alone device.

The main function of a NAS is file storage. But these kinds of devices have acquired other secondary features over the years.

History of NAS

Hard disks were invented by IBM in 1956, but it was only in 1983 that the world of computing began to offer a communication protocol allowing files to be read and written to another computer via a wired network: the "NetWare Core Protocol". Thus, the first NAS in history is the "NetWare" server from Novell.

The following year, in 1984, the company Sun Microsystems developed a similar protocol, NFS, which enables file sharing across a network. Then Microsoft also got involved with the product "LAN Manager".

In the early 1990s, 3com and Auspex Systems were the first companies to market dedicated NAS devices.

Gradually, the offer is growing and all companies and organizations are acquiring NAS to share files among their employees. Employees are increasingly discouraged from saving their files "locally" on their C partition because the NAS offers more flexibility for backup and sharing.

In the early 2000s, the NAS was introduced to individuals. It takes the form of a device that Internet service providers call a "box". The boxes are actually routers + TV set-top boxes + NAS.

Price

NAS costs about 300 to 400 Euros in 2017.

Connectivity

A NAS is a device that is permanently connected to your box as shown in this diagram:

PC   Router   NAS

Figure 36 : The three components of a modern home backup system

Since boxes and NAS are 24/7 devices, cyclical backups of your computer can be done in the background without your manual intervention.

If you're convinced of the benefits of NAS, you'll need to take a few steps to get there. First, you will need to know how much storage capacity you need. For example, 1TB, 2TB or even 8TB. The storage capacity you choose should anticipate your future needs. If you're short on 1 TB of disk space today, choose 2 TB right away.

Next, compare NAS manufacturer brands. There are at least 4 that trust the market.

- Synology
- Western Digital
- QNAP
- Asustor

Beware of buying a NAS with included hard drives, otherwise you'll get into a real mechanic's job to add the hard drives to it.

Then the installation of NAS is a delicate subject. They are very simple devices in appearance ... except on the day they are installed. Since each model works differently, it is impossible in this book to dwell on the steps involved in installing a home NAS. But here are the overall steps:

1. Connect the NAS to the box with a commonly supplied network cable.
2. Connect the NAS to the wall outlet.
3. Follow the "First Steps" manual provided in the package.
4. Set up cyclical backups of home computers.

Cyclical backups are the main reason a person wants to acquire a SIN. Either the manufacturer of the NAS provides cyclic backup tools or you will need to download more.

- Western Digital's cyclic backup tool is called *WD Sync*.
- QNAP's is called *QNAP NetBak Replicator*.
- Asustor's is called *Backup Plan*.
- Finally, Synology's is called *Cloud Station Backup*.

All in all, these products will ask you which folders you want to backup, how often, and will then apply themselves to performing the backups silently and regularly.

In addition, all these products work by incremental backup, i.e. they only back up files that have changed since the last backup. In doing so, each backup (except the first one) lasts only generally a few seconds or minutes.

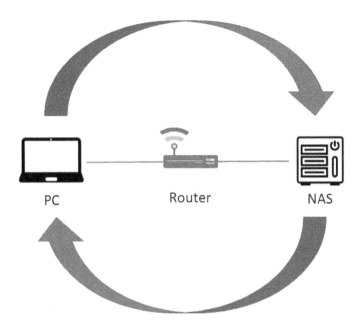

Figure 37 : PC and NAS exchanging files regularly in order to have identical files

Finally, for a few years now, NAS has been coming to the Clouds. Indeed, with almost all NAS, it is now possible to access your files outside your home thanks to a secure connection that goes through the box of your home.

- At Western Digital, the system is called "MyCloud".
- At Synology it's "Cloud Sync".
- At Asustor it is "myasustor".
- At QNAP it's "myQNAPcloud".

So, your files become accessible wherever you are in the world.

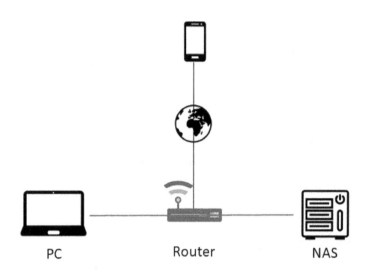

PC   Router   NAS

Figure 38 : Your NAS is accessible from outside your home

The smartphone

Let's be very direct: a smartphone can absolutely not be considered as a reliable storage place for your files.

A smartphone is a portable device which implies that it is at high risk of loss, theft or breakage. It is typically a "consumable" device: you buy it, you damage it, you drop it, you lose it, you buy it back in a cycle that lasts 12 to 18 months.

For this reason, it is necessary to remember to regularly save what is on it as photos and videos. Sometimes people cry like madeleines because a friend pushed them in a pool with their clothes on and their smartphone took the water and doesn't turn on again, losing more than six months of photos. Don't be like these people.

Figure 39 : A smartphone is not a reliable storage.

Depending on the system, Android or iPhone, you have several ways to back up your files.

iOS

To back up your files located on an iPhone, just plug your smartphone into a computer's USB port and unlock it. You'll then see a Windows explorer detailing a part of iOS tree. First, look in DCIM folder: you will find your photos and videos. You just have to copy and paste them to your computer's hard drive.

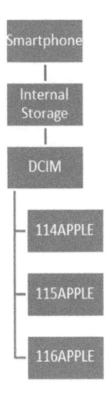

Figure 40 : iOS tree structure seen in Windows.

Android

To back up your files located on an Android phone, just plug your smartphone into a computer's USB port and unlock it. You'll then see a Windows explorer detailing the entire Android tree. First, look in DCIM folder: you will find your photos and videos. You just have to copy and paste them to your computer's hard drive.

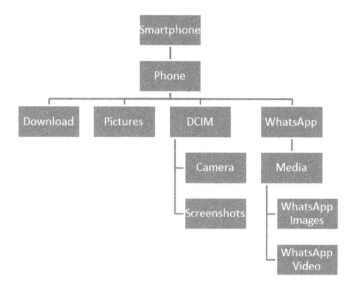

Figure 41 : Android tree structure seen in Windows.

Real-time backup of photos

More and more cloud hosting services and NAS manufacturers are offering applications to install in your smartphone to save every photo or video taken.

Try to get this kind of application: it will make your photos less vulnerable to the loss of your smartphone. Every time you take a photo, it will immediately go to a NAS or Cloud via 4G network or WIFI.

Figure 42 : Illustration of a smartphone that saves its photos by itself

This service is offered by NAS vendors, OneDrive, Google Drive, Dropbox and many others...

The copy cycle

As we have seen, all backup media are fallible. They can all disappoint you. This may seem like a gloomy view of computing, but it's true: no storage medium is perfect. So, what can you do?

The solution lies in **successive copies**, as the documentary "Do our computers have short memory?" indicates. That is, make sure you always have two (or more) identical data sets. Typically, you need a primary and a secondary storage location. As soon as the data from one is lost, you need to immediately rebuild it.

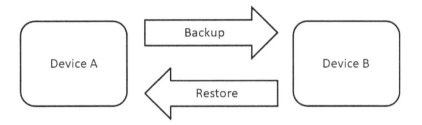

Figure 43 : File copy cycle

Every time your computer dies, you will buy another one and you will take your files back to the backup media of your choice.

On the other hand, each time your backup media fails (theft, breakage, loss, malfunction, ...), you will restore it from your computer data.

Warning: this system also has a flaw. If your computer and your backup device are in the same place, you can lose everything in case of a house fire or burglary.

Either you accept this risk or you reinforce your fire and antitheft systems. Or you may need to host your backup outside your home.

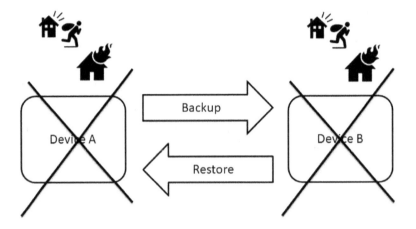

Figure 44 : A proper spatial distance is required to avoid that a fire or burglary makes disappear device A and device B at the same event

Manual copy vs synchronization

Manual copy-paste

Regardless of the storage medium chosen for your backups, you can always use the good old copy and paste method to duplicate your files or folders. It's very simple, everyone knows how to do it: you select the folders or files you want to backup and copy-drag them to the storage media (USB flash drive, external hard drive, ...).

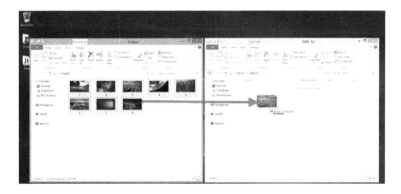

Figure 45 : In case you want to back up files from a PC to another device, you must copy and paste your files. Not drag and drop.

But the problem with this method is that the second time you try to do it, several files will already exist on the backup media. Windows will warn you that copying will cause errors.

This is why it is necessary to use a comparison and synchronization tool.

Comparison and synchronization

File comparison and synchronization are techniques for determining which files have changed since the last backup. The comparison will go through your original files and your backed-up files and compare them one by one to determine what needs to be done. Then the synchronization step is the one that will actually perform the copies or deletions.

A good example of synchronization software is FreeFileSync. It is free and can be downloaded from https://www.freefilesync.org/.

Here is an example of how FreeFileSync works: the software is composed of two panes. Each pane displays the files which are non-existent or different from the other side. They each represent a storage device, for example, a PC on the left (Drive Letter C) and an external disk drive on the right (Drive Letter D).

The first time the storage medium is used, it is still empty, as shown in this example:

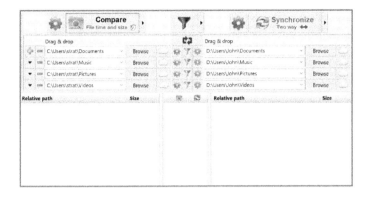

Figure 46 : Left and right panes, before any comparison of files

On the previous figure, you can see that 4 couples of directories are being compared.

`C:\Users\strat\Documents is compared with D:\Users\John\Documents.`

`C:\Users\strat\Music is compared with D:\Users\John\Music.`

`C:\Users\strat\Pictures is compared with D:\Users\John\Pictures.`

`C:\Users\strat\Videos is compared with D:\Users\John\Videos.`

If we launch the comparison, we can observe the differences between the constituants of each pair.

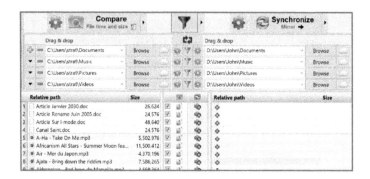

Figure 47 : The green arrows with a "+" indicate that these files must be copied from the PC (left) to the backup media (right).

Now, just press "Synchronize" to launch the backup. Then wait for the end of the copy.

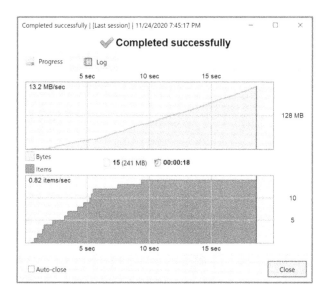

Figure 48 : End of copy

Next, time, only the modifications that has occurred since, will be detected by the comparison.

The Cloud

Presentation

A word that has become very fashionable in recent years, the "Cloud" is the concept that brings together all forms of exploitation of the storage capacities of remote computer servers via the Internet network. This concept owes its name to the word cloud in English. The man who invented this term in 1996 is called George Favaloro. He is an employee of the Compaq company who wrote a memo in 1996 telling his colleagues that "The Internet will have a profound impact on Compaq's customers. He suggested that his company anticipate that many services currently performed by the devices owned by customers are migrating to the Internet cloud.

Since 1977, computer scientists have been using the drawing of a small cloud to represent the Internet because it allows them to quickly draw a simple way to say "several computers connected by Internet without specifying their geographical location".

Figure 49 : On computer sketches, since 1977, the cloud has meant "several computers whose geographical location is unknown".

In recent years, high-speed Internet connections for individuals and businesses have transformed the world into a vast information superhighway. Even the largest files can travel from point A to point B on the planet in the blink of an eye.

In France, the average internet speed is 8.9 Mbps... far behind our neighbors.

Fiber is good, it's cool, it's fast and most of all it's... not accessible to everyone. According to an Akamai study, the average internet speed in France is only 8.9 Mbps, which is very low compared to most of our European neighbors. [...]

Figure 50 : Excerpt from an article published on 30/03/2016 (on http://www.cnetfrance.fr)

Even if we consider the average internet speed as low, 8.9 Mbps still means that a 1-megabyte file takes on average 1 second to reach its destination with most of the French internet connections. This transfer speed has enabled the democratization of remote file hosting services such as Dropbox or Google Drive.

Figure 51 : Logos of the main players in the cloud file storage market.

These companies offer, free of charge or against payment, to keep a copy of your files in their servers without telling you where they are located. For commercial and security reasons, no file hosting company specifies where its servers are located. Most consumers don't want to know that.

Perhaps the cloud should, after all, be represented not by a cloud but by a big question mark.

In reality, the storage facilities are large air-conditioned warehouses in which hundreds of computers resembling large cabinets are lined up.

These warehouses store multiple versions of your files in duplicate or even triple versions. In the event of a fire in one of these warehouses, you probably wouldn't even know about it for two reasons:

- Another warehouse identical to the first one would take over thanks to the backup copy of your files,
- The company, to protect its brand image would do everything to ensure that you never learn of the destruction of its premises.

In IT lingo, these large warehouses are called **datacenters**. They are large, heavy, energy-intensive and loaded with computer equipment. Their doors are well guarded and their walls are armored. This is the exact opposite of the "cloud" image associated with them.

Figure 52 : A datacenter is like a huge warehouse.

Figure 53 : Customer data is stored on hard drives stacked in these large computer cabinets that are on 24/7.

These companies put in place a lot of technological controls to ensure two crucial things for their customers:

- Archiving files for as long as possible,
- Availability of files at any time of the day or night.

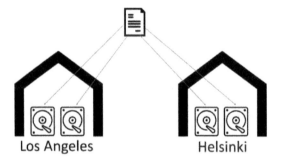

Los Angeles   Helsinki

Figure 54 : Thanks to hard disk redundancy and data center redundancy, your files exist in multiple locations and therefore remain available with excellent reliability even in the event of a disaster.

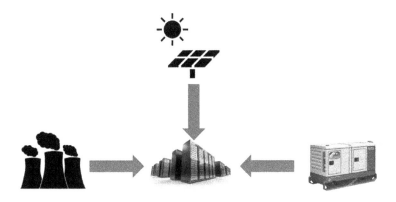

Figure 55 : Datacenters are very energy-intensive places. They are directly connected to powerful power plants, as well as to renewable energy sources in order to give a "green" image to their service. Finally, most of them are also equipped with diesel generator

Despite all the precautions taken by online storage companies, it is worth remembering that you should always have a copy of all the files you upload to them. The attitude of having nothing on your computer and sending everything to the cloud would be stupid.

Think again about the copy cycle.

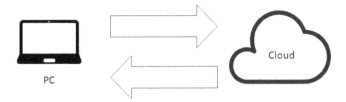

Figure 56 : If your computer crashes, the cloud will return all your files. Conversely, if the cloud fails, all your files will already be at home on your computer.

Why would the cloud fail?

For a variety of reasons.

- Subscription terminated for non-payment.
- Global service failure of the hosting provider.
- Network connection outage from your side.
- Failure of the internet infrastructure located between the datacenter and you.
- Destruction of the datacenter (war, earthquake, tornado...)

However, under normal circumstances, we must admit that these services work very well and make your data ubiquitous.

What are the advantages of cloud hosting services?

1. **Ubiquity**. Your files are available anywhere in the world and on all types of devices such as smartphones, tablets and computers.
2. **Immediate availability**. Unlike USB flash drives or external hard drives that require manual plugging in, Cloud services are always available without any human action on your part.
3. **No material risk to you**. Although no one wants to experience a burglary, water damage or fire at home, having their files copied to a cloud is a form of insurance against these losses.
4. **Flexible storage**. As you add more files, you simply subscribe to a higher package to get more storage space from the hosting provider.

How much does it cost?

Prices are quite different from one hosting provider to another because they compete fiercely for your data. Here are some examples of pricing in November 2020.

Google drive prices:

Capacity	*15 GB*	*100 GB*	*200 GB*
Price	Free	1.99 €/month	2.99 €/month

OneDrive drive prices:

Capacity	*5 GB*	*100 GB*	*1 TB*
Price	Free	2 €/month	69 €/year

Dropbox prices:

Capacity	*2 TB*	*3 TB*	*5 TB*
Price	9.99 €/month	16.58 €/month	10 €/user/month

Amazon Drive prices:

Capacity	5 GB	100 GB	1 TB
Price	Free	1.99 €/month	9.99 €/month

How to subscribe?

It's quite simple: go to the website of one of the file hosting companies (there are hundreds of them) and look for the words "subscribe", "subscribe", "subscribe", etc...

Beforehand, do not hesitate to compare the offers, and read the special conditions.

And if you want to play the patriotic card, find out if the service datacenters are located in France. For example, the company OpenHost has chosen to offer only datacenter hosting on the French territory.

Getting started with your cloud hosting service

Once you have subscribed to a cloud hosting service, you get storage space from your hosting provider. This storage space is accessible through a URL address.

For example, https://drive.google.com/drive/my-drive for Google Drive:

Figure 57 : For the moment there is no file

Another example is https://onedrive.live.com for Microsoft OneDrive:

Figure 58 : For the moment there is no file

You now need to install the small module to synchronize your files. It is a program that will run regularly on your computer to reflect in real time all your creations, modifications and deletions of files to the Cloud.

To get this synchronizer, you shouldn't have any difficulty: Microsoft OneDrive's synchronizer already exists on all Windows 8 or 10 computers worldwide.

For others, look for the "Get Applications" or "Download Drive for PC" links, usually at the bottom left of web pages.

For example, at Google Drive, you get this page: https://www.google.com/drive/download/

Figure 59 : Google Drive download page for PCs

Click on "Download for PC" to obtain the following installation file:

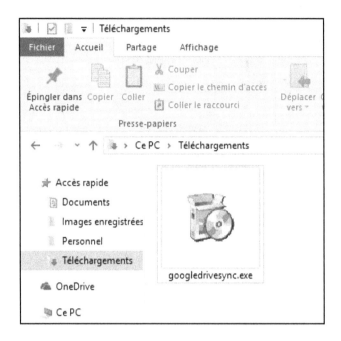

Figure 60 : For PC, the sofware to install is a small EXE

Double-click on it to install it and then follow the installation wizard.

At some point, you will be asked for your account login and password in order to authenticate your connection to the Cloud.

Once logged in, Google Drive, tells you that a folder "Google Drive" has been created on your computer. From now on it is this folder that will provide the synchronization gateway between your computer and the cloud. Everything in this folder will also be in the cloud and vice versa.

Procedure is the same for OneDrive.

Figure 61 : The first time you put files and folders in the cloud folder on your PC, they will immediately upload to the corresponding cloud.

Warning: it is up to you to know if you have subscribed to sufficient space for all your files. If you exceed the space allocated to you in the cloud, you risk either a malfunction or a price increase. Be sure to measure the size of your files before you subscribe.

Now, feel free to drag and drop your four folders - Music, Documents, Videos, and Pictures - to the cloud folder (Google Drive folder, OneDrive, or Dropbox, whatever).

Attention: for OneDrive, at the end of the installation on Windows, your Documents and Pictures are automatically moved to OneDrive! They don't wait for your opinion!

Figure 62 : Move your existing folders inside the cloud provider folder. (Not copy ! Move.)

When a file or folder is on its way to the Cloud, you will see a small blue circle on its icon:

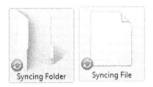

Figure 63 : Folder being synchronized

At the end, if the folder or file icon has a small green check mark then it means that the synchronization is complete and therefore the file or folder is exactly the same on the computer and in the cloud.

Ready Folder   Ready File

Figure 64 : Fully synchronized folder

The synchronization time depends on the speed of your internet connection and the size of the files you have. It can therefore take a minute, an hour, a day, a week...

It is strongly discouraged to have a DSL connection to use Cloud hosting. It is too slow. Fiber or DOCSIS (internet by cable) are the best choices.

Once the synchronization is complete, you will find that your files have all landed in the Cloud:

Figure 65 : Web view of your space at Google Drive

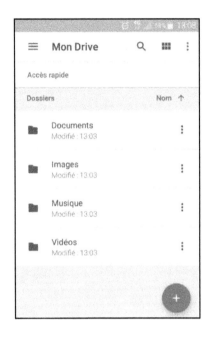

Figure 66 : Android view of your Google Drive space

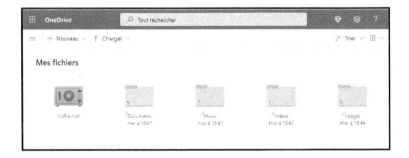

Figure 67 : Web view of your space at OneDrive

Figure 68 : View from OneDrive app

All you have to do is use your files as you did before. Anything that happens to them will be reflected in the Cloud.

Action	Repercussion in the cloud
Creating a file	Creation of the file in the cloud
Renaming a file	Renaming the file in the cloud
Moving a file	Moving the file to the cloud
Editing a file	Modification + versioning
Deleting a file	Trashing

Versions

Thanks to versioning, you will be able to find the old versions of each file. This is handy if you have accidentally changed a sentence in a Word document and can't remember what was marked before.

To do this, go to the web page of your hosting service and right-click on the file and enter the "Manage versions" menu:

Figure 69 : Version management in Google Drive

And how to change host?

As with any service you subscribe to, it is possible to cancel and switch to a competitor. The procedure is really simple.

1. First of all, take out a new subscription with competitor X.
2. Download and install the X synchronization software on your PC.
3. Move the entire contents of the folder on your current host to the X folder.

Automatically, the host you had before will put all your files in the recycle garbage can and won't synchronize them anymore. On the other hand, your new host, X, will copy all your files to its cloud.

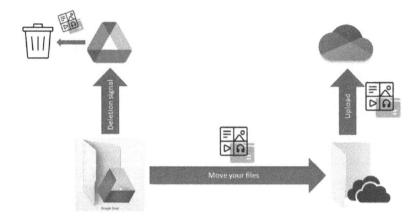

Figure 70 : To switch to a new cloud host, just move your files from cloud folder A to cloud folder B on your PC

Restore a backup

Throughout this book, techniques for backing up system or user files have been discussed. It is now time to learn how to use these backups in the event of a disaster. There are several possible scenarios.

WARNING: If you are not comfortable with unusual computer manipulations, do not launch yourself and contact a computer repairman, or enforce the warranty of your device!

If you have accidentally lost or modified a file

This is the simplest situation: connect to your backup device and search for the file and then take it back with a simple copy and paste.

If your computer has been stolen or lost

In this situation, you will have to start by buying a new computer, preferably with the same operating system as the previous one (Windows or MacOS).

As the device will be brand new and totally different from the previous one, system backups will not help you at all. Just turn on the new computer and connect it to your user file backup device (cloud, NAS, USB stick, CD, DVD, or external hard drive).

Then manually copy the desired files from the backup to the new computer.

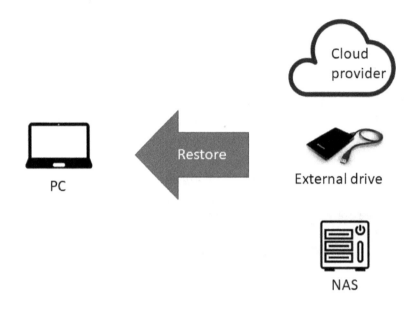

Cloud provider

Restore

PC

External drive

NAS

Figure 71 : Manual restoration is simple: log onto a NAS or a cloud drive, or plug in an external drive and you can get your files back.

If your computer has been damaged (water, fire, breakage)

You can either take your device to a data recovery lab, a computer repair shop, or buy a new computer.

If the repairer or lab is able to get your computer up and running again, you may not need a backup. But if they don't, you're just like the previous case.

If your computer is a victim of a virus or if Windows stops booting

This is typically the case when Windows needs to be restored.

<u>Warning: the operations described below may change from one version of Windows to another and may change the sequence without this book being updated. Again, if you are not comfortable, let a professional restore your device for you.</u>

Insert a Windows Repair CD into the CD drive and restart. If your computer does not have an optical drive, you will need either an external CD drive to connect to USB or another computer to copy the repair CD to a USB stick.

OR

Go into the search box of windows and type "update" in order to open the Windows Update panel.

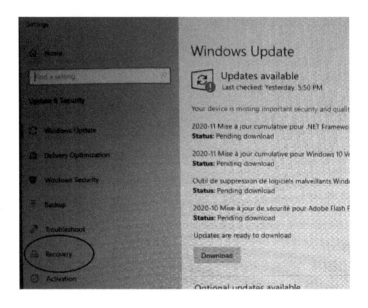

Figure 72 : Click on "Recovery" (on the left).

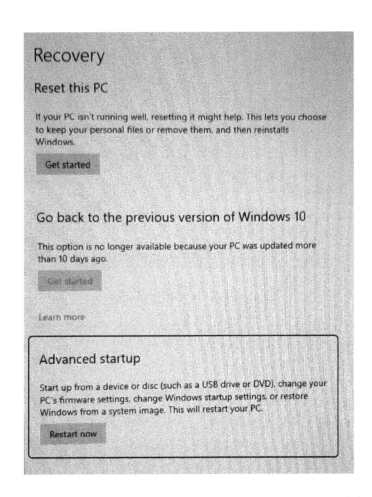

Figure 73 : Then, click on "Restart now". The computer will boot again and show a blue menu.

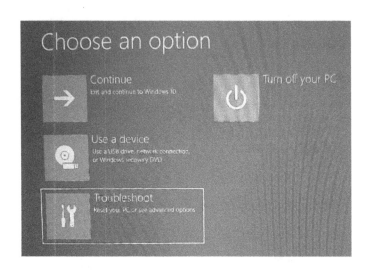

Figure 74 : Click on Troubleshoot

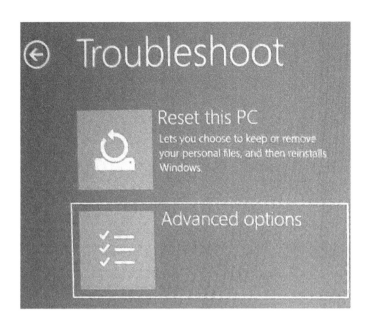

Figure 75 : Click on Advanced options

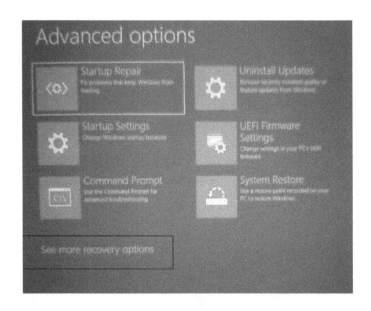

Figure 76 : Click on "See more recovery options"

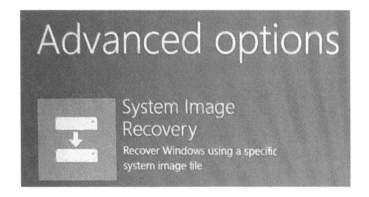

Figure 77 : Click on System Image Recovery

Figure 78 : Now, plug in your external device containing the system backup then follow the next steps. At the end, your computer will be the same as the day you had performed the backup.

That's all.

Conclusion

This book has tried to get you into the very open club of people who back up their computer files. The reader of this book will no doubt remember that no backup system is infallible or free, but that it is better to try to back up than to do nothing at all.

NAS, cloud hosting services, and external hard drives are the top three backup modes.

- NAS are expensive to purchase but are free to use. They require a bit of configuration, which will tend to put off the general public a bit. However, they guarantee a home storage of all your files.

- Cloud hosting services are the easiest solutions to implement because there is no hardware to buy. On the other hand, they entail monthly or annual user fees. These services have a great opacity and do not allow to know where the files are geographically located.

- The external hard drive is an inexpensive hardware allowing large storage capacities. Easy to use, it is also unfortunately easy to lose or steal. Apart from the high risk of breakage when falling, they are rather robust.

Backup frequency is also a key element of its efficiency: if you don't back up your data often, it's as if you don't do anything.

Finally, backup can be an opportunity to make your data more ubiquitous: always accessible in your pocket. Not only are your files in a safe place and therefore will follow you throughout your life, but they will follow you wherever you go!

References

http://www.futura-sciences.com/tech/actualites/informatique-cd-dvd-enregistrables-sont-tres-mauvais-supports-archivage-23209/

http://www.latribune.fr/actualites/economie/20131129trib000798527/en-jetant-son-vieil-ordinateur-il-perd-plus-de-7-millions-de-dollars-en-bitcoins.html

http://france3-regions.francetvinfo.fr/hauts-de-france/on-vole-son-ordinateur-photos-son-mari-decede-sa-famille-lance-appel-facebook-1227933.html

http://www.ipwatchdog.com/2016/05/11/micro-economic-estimate-reasonable-royalty-rate-standard-essential-patents/id=68827/

https://fr.wikipedia.org/wiki/Disquette

https://fr.wikipedia.org/wiki/Disque_compact_enregistrable

https://fr.wikipedia.org/wiki/Disque_dur

https://en.wikipedia.org/wiki/Magnetic_tape_data_storage

http://www.lefigaro.fr/secteur/high-tech/2015/02/02/32001-20150202ARTFIG00165-lameilleure-solution-pour-sauvegarder-vos-fichiers-informatiques.php

http://www.arte.tv/fr/videos/050717-000-A/nos-ordinateurs-ont-ils-la-memoire-courte

https://fr.wikipedia.org/wiki/Cloud_computing

http://www.cnetfrance.fr/news/en-france-le-debit-internet-moyen-est-de-89-mbps-loin-derriere-nos-voisins-39834836.htm

https://gigaom.com/2011/08/22/the-latest-leed-platinum-data-center-courtesy-of-vantage/

http://www.datacenterknowledge.com/solar-powered-data-centers/

https://www.lesechos.fr/tech-medias/hightech/0212076838259-une-centaine-de-pays-touches-par-une-cyberattaque-mondiale-2086484.php

https://lecrabeinfo.net/creer-image-systeme-windows-10-8-7.html

https://www.openhost-network.com/choisir-hebergement-cloud-france/

http://www.iphon.fr/post/tuto-pratique-ios-5-comment-faire-synchro-sans-fil-iphone-ipod-touch

https://www.freefilesync.org/

www.ingramcontent.com/pod-product-compliance
Lightning Source LLC
Chambersburg PA
CBHW070847070326
40690CB00009B/1731